ADRIANA LUNA CARLOS

Editor-In-Chief, Designer and Co-Founder

HANNA OLIVAS

Managing Editor & Co-Founder

BECOMING AN UNSTOPPABLE
WOMAN

MAGAZINE

SHE RISES
S T U D I O S

ADVERTISING OPPORTUNITIES

Info@SheRisesStudios.com

BAUW MAGAZINE *DECEMBER 2023*

CONTACT US

SheRisesStudios@gmail.com
www.SheRisesStudios.com

www.SheRisesStudios.com

LETTER FROM THE EDITORS

Dear Readers,

This November, we're diving deep into a theme that's close to our hearts: "Self-Worth and Manifestation: Building a Life You Love."

In a world that often measures success by external standards, it's easy to lose sight of our inherent worthiness. We are here to remind you that you are enough, just as you are. Your worthiness is not defined by your achievements, your appearance, or the opinions of others. It's a birthright, an unwavering truth, and the cornerstone upon which you can build the life you've always dreamt of.

As you flip through the pages of this issue, you'll discover the profound connection between self-worth and the art of manifestation. Self-worth isn't an optional accessory; it's the foundation upon which all your dreams and desires can be built. When you believe in yourself, the universe aligns to help you achieve your goals.

Throughout this issue, you'll encounter the real stories of remarkable women who have harnessed the power of self-worth and manifestation to shape their destinies. They've faced challenges, conquered doubts, and emerged as the architects of their own lives. Their journeys are a testament to the incredible potential that resides within each of us.

This November, embrace your worthiness, trust in your ability to manifest, and set forth on a journey of self-discovery and creation. As always, we're here to accompany you every step of the way.

Thank you for being part of our community, for sharing your stories, and for believing in the unstoppable potential within us all.

With boundless love and empowerment,

P.S. Remember, your worthiness is the key that unlocks the door to the life you love.

Adriana Luna Carlos and Hanna Olivas
Editors of Becoming an Unstoppable Woman Magazine

Rise

with Hanna Olivas

In the realm of motivational speakers and business coaches, few stories resonate as powerfully as that of **Bershan Shaw**. A sought-after international speaker, business coach, women's advocate, and author, Bershan's journey to success has been marked by dedication, perseverance, and a profound encounter with mortality.

Bershan's remarkable story began with a life-altering diagnosis – she was a two-time breast cancer survivor facing a daunting three-month prognosis. Faced with the imminent threat of losing her battle against cancer, Bershan made the decision to summon her inner warrior, embarking on a journey to conquer the impossible, defy the odds, and ultimately triumph over her illness.

Now, armed with the lessons learned from her personal struggle, Bershan channels her leadership skills into motivating others to reach their full potential. Her no-nonsense approach is a testament to her resilience and determination, qualities she believes are essential for overcoming life's challenges.

Bershan's impact extends beyond the motivational stage; she actively coaches executives and trains teams across diverse industries, including financial services, legal, technology, and consumer products. Her ability to inspire and lead has made her a sought-after figure in the professional development arena.

Her media appearances on **NBC, ABC, Fox, and OWN** have further amplified her message of resilience and empowerment. Through these platforms, Bershan shares her story, encouraging others to confront adversity head-on and turn challenges into opportunities for growth.

Recognition for Bershan's contributions has poured in from various quarters. Her accolades include a BET Trailblazer award, the 2017 Woman Whole Life Achievement Award, Business & Leadership of Excellence from Woman Economic Forum, and the 2017 Lifetime Achievement Award for National and Community Service from the President of the United States.

URAWARRIOR

A proud graduate of New York University with a master's degree in journalism and business, Bershan's commitment to continuous learning is evident. She also holds a certificate in leadership and executive coaching from the same institution, underscoring her dedication to honing her skills and knowledge.

Bershan's impact transcends geographical boundaries; currently splitting her time between New York, LA, and Washington, DC, she embodies the spirit of a global influencer. Her ability to connect with diverse audiences stems from her genuine passion for empowering individuals to overcome obstacles and thrive in their personal and professional lives.

Beyond her role as a motivational force, Bershan is a tech founder, spearheading the URA Warrior app. This innovative platform focuses on mental health, providing resources and support to help both men and women prioritize their mental, physical, and emotional well-being. Through this initiative, Bershan aims to foster human connection and create a community that thrives on mutual support.

As a breast cancer survivor, Bershan Shaw stands as a beacon of hope for those facing adversity. Her journey from the brink of despair to becoming a global motivator and business coach is a testament to the transformative power of resilience, determination, and the indomitable human spirit. In the face of life's challenges, Bershan continues to inspire others to embrace their inner warriors and strive for success against all odds.

Watch the full episode here: https://fenixtv.app/programs/

A Year of Transformation:
Marissa Warren's Journey and Year-End Reflections

In every life, there comes a moment, a turning point, when one realizes the profound impact of their work on the lives of others. For Marissa Warren, that moment arrives daily. She's not just a hypnotherapist and transformational consultant; she's the beacon of hope for those who have tried everything else and find themselves at the crossroads of change.

Describing a single defining moment is a formidable task, as Marissa has been instrumental in life-altering transformations. Her clients have experienced miracles, from the birth of healthy babies to reclaiming lives on the brink of despair. Yet, it's not only the monumental shifts that mark her journey. It's the smaller, incremental changes—the mending of boundaries, healing ancestral trauma, nurturing the inner child, conquering addictions, fostering positive mindsets, and crafting a better daily life—that truly make her work remarkable.

In Marissa's world, clients are the compass guiding every decision. She continually asks herself, "How can I enhance their experience? How can I enable deeper healing and higher elevation?" Her mission is clear: Inspire, Success, Elevate. At its core, it's about inspiring through actions, words, and insights, paving the way for others to step up and make transformative changes in their lives.

Empowerment for Marissa encompasses not just her own success, but creating an environment where others can achieve their personal victories. She dedicates herself to helping others elevate their mind, body, and soul, propelling them to new heights of inner growth and personal transformation.

Each workday brings something different, a unique session, presenting a variety of challenges. This diversity fuels her passion. Every day, she anticipates the unexpected, working with what arises and empowering her clients to tap into their inner power for enduring change.

In today's business landscape, women entrepreneurs face distinct challenges—a relentless inner critic, imposter syndrome, and the exhaustion of trying to be everything to everyone. A never-ending to-do list, the comparison trap, and analysis paralysis often overshadow their desire for personal and professional growth. It's tempting to stay in the comfort zone, but Marissa knows women are destined for more.

In her world, the perception of life and experiences determines their outcomes. Changing the internal world changes the external world. By uncovering and releasing limitations, false narratives, and negative inner beliefs,

Marissa empowers her clients to create new realities and dialogues. The rewiring of minds and the subconscious facilitates a fast track to change.

But mindset alone isn't enough. It's about taking inspired and aligned action. She believes that implementing inner mindset work through action is key to real transformation. The integration of this work is supported by journaling, providing a reference point for staying on course.

As Marissa emphasizes, life's outcome relies on perceptions, driven by the internal belief system. Changing thoughts changes experiences. It's not merely a philosophy but a profound practice that brings tangible results. Marissa draws an analogy—changing mental patterns is like reprogramming a GPS; new directions yield new destinations.

Self-care is a formula: grounding, centering, integration. Grounding techniques reduce stress and create stability. Centering involves balance and calm, a return to inner equilibrium. Integration fuses physical, emotional, and mental aspects, promoting unity and balance. This formula ensures she navigates life's challenges with resilience and connection.

As for grounding, Marissa begins her day with meditation, allowing her to connect with the present moment and foster stability. Centering is achieved through breathwork, providing emotional and mental balance. Integration involves implementation, the doing of the work, and the embodiment of her mission. Through these practices, she maintains her well-being, gracefully managing the dual roles of professional and personal responsibilities.

Her daily rituals keep her centered, balanced, and vibrating at a high frequency. Her key to success lies in living her formula—grounding, centering, integration—every single day.

Marissa relies on a strong support system built within her network, emphasizing the importance of like-minded connections with varied skill sets. She encourages aspiring women entrepreneurs to cultivate similar networks, focusing on collaboration over competition. By working together, unity empowers all.

Remaining at the forefront of her industry, Marissa prioritizes continuous evolution. She believes that staying true to her core mission, delivering exceptional experiences, and aligning with her areas of expertise are essential. She highlights the importance of staying authentic and true to one's vision, avoiding the trap of comparing oneself to others.

Personal and professional development is intrinsically linked to inner growth and transformation. The practice of delving deep within oneself, facing every aspect, and shedding light on the shadows has been profoundly impactful. As she discovered, once you explore your inner world, facing external challenges becomes easier.

As Marissa continues to inspire and uplift others, the most rewarding aspect is witnessing the ripple effect of her clients' transformations. As clients navigate one area of transformation, it inevitably affects other areas of their lives, creating lasting, lifelong changes.

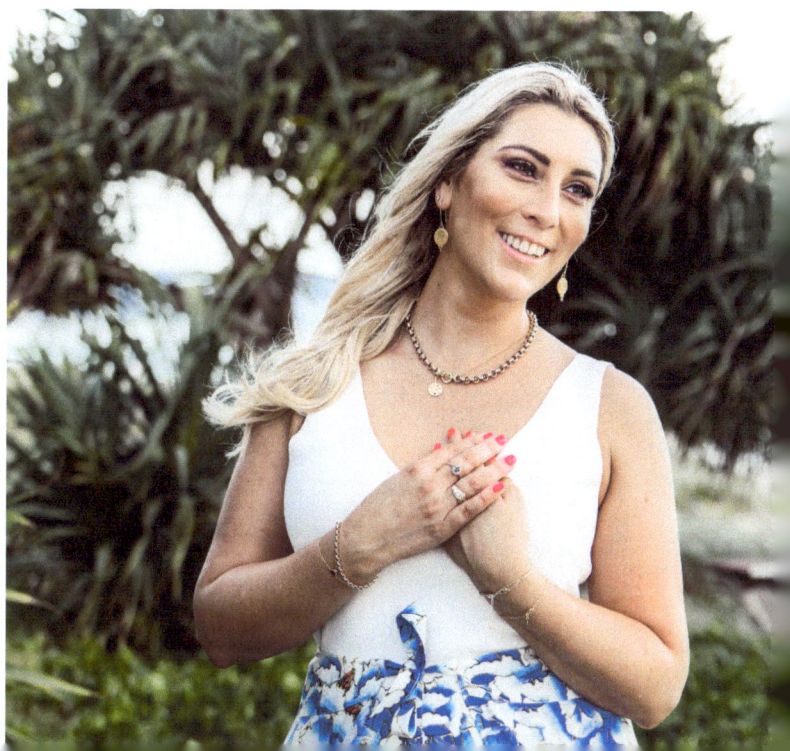

WOMEN ON THE

Rise

RISING STRONGER: A WOMAN'S JOURNEY TO TRIUMPH IN LIFE AND BUSINESS AFTER UNEXPECTED HEALTH CHALLENGES

Written by Nicole Curtis

Life is a journey filled with unexpected twists and turns, and sometimes, it throws challenges our way that seem insurmountable. For many women, health issues can be a formidable obstacle, impacting both personal and professional spheres. I know this struggle intimately, having faced my own health challenges. However, I am living proof that it is possible to rise stronger than ever, not only in life but also in the demanding arena of business. In this article, I share my personal journey and the top three ways that can help women return stronger than ever after dealing with health issues.

Embrace Resilience as Your Superpower

The first step in rising stronger is to embrace resilience as your superpower. Resilience is not the absence of struggle, but the ability to bounce back from adversity. My own health challenges became a pivotal moment in my life, forcing me to confront my vulnerability and discover the reservoirs of strength within me. Resilience is not a trait we are born with; it is a skill that can be developed and refined through life's experiences.

To cultivate resilience, it's crucial to acknowledge and accept your emotions. Allow yourself to feel the pain, frustration, and even moments of despair. However, don't let these emotions define you. Instead, use them as stepping stones toward resilience. Seek support from loved ones, connect with a mentor, or join a community of women who have faced similar challenges. Sharing your story not only helps you heal but also inspires others to find strength in their vulnerabilities.

Prioritize Self-Care Without Guilt

As women, we often find ourselves juggling multiple responsibilities, both at home and in the workplace. When health issues arise, it becomes imperative to prioritize self-care without guilt. Society may project the image of a superwoman who can handle it all, but the truth is, that we are human, and our bodies require care and attention.

Returning stronger after health challenges involves redefining self-care as a non-negotiable aspect of your routine. This means listening to your body, getting enough rest, nourishing yourself with wholesome foods, and engaging in activities that bring you joy. For me, my favorite activity that brings me joy is hanging out with my chickens and collecting eggs. It's not selfish to put your well-being first; in fact, it is an essential investment in your ability to navigate life and business with resilience and strength.

Delegate tasks and responsibilities when needed, whether at home or in the workplace. Surround yourself with a support system that understands and encourages your commitment to self-care. Remember, you cannot pour from an empty cup. By prioritizing your well-being, you are not only healing but also laying the foundation for a stronger, more vibrant version of yourself.

Leverage the Power of Adaptability

Life seldom follows a linear path, and health challenges can disrupt even the most carefully laid plans. Embracing adaptability is the third key to rising stronger. Instead of viewing detours as setbacks, consider them opportunities for growth and transformation. My own journey taught me that adaptability is not a sign of weakness but a testament to our ability to evolve.

Approach challenges with a growth mindset, recognizing that setbacks can pave the way for comebacks. This perspective shift is a powerful tool for navigating both personal and professional challenges. In the business world, adaptability is often the differentiating factor between those who merely survive and those who thrive.

Developing adaptability involves honing problem-solving skills, staying open to new possibilities, and cultivating a mindset that embraces change as a natural part of life. Seek out opportunities for continuous learning and skill development, both personally and professionally. By becoming adaptable, you not only weather the storms of life more gracefully but also position yourself as a resilient leader in the business arena.

Conclusion

Life's challenges, particularly health issues, can be formidable adversaries. However, they also present an opportunity for profound personal and professional growth. My journey is a testament to the fact that it is possible to rise stronger than ever, not in spite of health challenges but because of them.

Embracing resilience as your superpower, prioritizing self-care without guilt, and leveraging the power of adaptability are the three pillars that can help women return stronger after facing health issues. As you navigate your unique journey, remember that strength is not the absence of vulnerability but the courage to rise in the face of it. By embracing these principles, you have the potential not only to overcome challenges but to emerge as a powerful force, ready to thrive in both life and business.

facebook.com/nicolecurtiscrazychickenlady

@nicolecurtiscrazychickenlady

Krystal Casey: A Beacon of Empowerment and Resilience

Krystal Casey is a remarkable individual who has risen above personal adversity to become a guiding light in the realms of self-care and self-empowerment. Her story is one of transformation, resilience, and unwavering strength. After enduring years of traditional treatment for mental and emotional trauma, Krystal discovered the transformative power of yoga. She embarked on a journey of self-discovery and healing, eventually opening her own yoga studio. However, her life took a drastic turn when her husband faced charges of sexual abuse against a minor and tragically passed away.

A Journey of Healing and Resilience

Krystal's life was shattered by the unimaginable loss and trauma she experienced. The weight of grief and trauma was immense, but she found the strength to persevere for the sake of her five children. Recognizing that she couldn't let the cycles of trauma continue, Krystal decided to be an example for her children, demonstrating how to rise above unspeakable hardships.

Through months of dedicated self-care, self-intimacy, and self-empowerment, Krystal discovered a newfound resilience and inner strength. She emerged from the ashes of her past, transformed and empowered. Today, Krystal Casey is on a mission to help other mothers find their voices, reignite their inner spark, and create lives that truly light them up. She is a passionate advocate for breaking generational cycles, offering support, guidance, and empowerment to mothers as they navigate the challenges of motherhood and life itself.

Empowering Others Through Authorship and Coaching

As an author, instructor, and empowerment coach, Krystal has made it her life's mission to inspire and uplift others. She shares her experiences, wisdom, and insights to empower women to harness their feminine power. Krystal's story serves as a powerful reminder that adversity can be overcome, and one can emerge from the darkest of times with newfound strength and purpose.

The Womanhood Anthology: A Guiding Light

Krystal Casey is a pivotal contributor to the "Womanhood: Identity to Intimacy and Everything in Between" anthology. This transformative book dares to explore sensitive and often taboo topics related to womanhood. It delves into intimate aspects of being a woman, addressing issues that are often shrouded in silence and shame. Through candid conversations and insightful tools, this anthology offers a lifeline to those seeking comfort, understanding, and empowerment.

The anthology is divided into several parts, each focusing on a different facet of womanhood. It provides a platform for remarkable women to share their stories of resilience, vulnerability, and growth. "Womanhood" is more than just a collection of stories; it is a vital resource and manual for women who may not have had anyone to talk to about these sensitive issues. Krystal Casey, along with her fellow contributors, aims to empower women, validate their experiences, and redefine the narrative of womanhood.

A Collective Sisterhood of Empowerment

Krystal Casey's work, both in her personal journey and as an author and coach, reflects the power of authentic conversations and the strength of vulnerability. Through her storytelling and advocacy, she encourages women to embrace their unique journeys, celebrate their resilience, and cherish the connections they make along the way.

Krystal Casey's story is a testament to the human spirit's ability to rise from adversity, find strength in vulnerability, and empower others through shared experiences. She is a beacon of hope and inspiration for widows, mothers, and women everywhere, demonstrating that they are never alone and that there is always hope for a brighter tomorrow.

---

https://www.flightofthephoenixcollective.com/

Together We Rise: A Call to Women

By Julianne Williams

I am inherently a bold and determined woman - one deeply involved in the business world, devoted to championing my fellow women, and committed to challenging societal norms to establish a secure and equitable environment for all. The authentic struggles of women are comprehended most intimately by our own.

My mission is clear: to stand as the strongest advocate for women and cultivate a community rooted in mutual upliftment. Here are a few cherished approaches through which I extend encouragement and support to my fellow women:"

1. Show Up for Them

Extend your presence in various forms – a daily uplifting text, a comforting call, a supportive listener in times of distress, acknowledgment of her strength, backing women-led startups, or simply sharing a smile over a meal or during shopping. Be an advocate and a cheerleader, recognizing that the most valuable gift we can give is our time and emotional investment in one another.

2. Create Safe Spaces

Cultivate openness about challenges, family matters, triumphs, and vulnerabilities. Secrecy can breed jealousy and animosity, as the unknown fosters insecurity in the human experience. Acknowledge imperfections, share both joyful and challenging experiences, empower each other, and ensure no one feels excluded or alienated

3. Embrace Your Journey

Recognize jealousy as a negative emotion, stemming from natural but sometimes unfounded comparisons. Whether it's financial success, physical attributes, or relationships, remember that appearances can be deceiving. Counteract negativity by expressing gratitude for your own blessings, and understanding that joy is preserved when we appreciate both ourselves and others.

Comparing our lives to others will only steal our joy.

Always remember that when we feel good about ourselves and others, we start attracting good things in our lives.

4. Let Empathy Be Your Guide

All humans have a natural tendency to judge others for their past and life choices. Resist the inclination to form opinions about others of their past or choices. Instead of scrutinizing someone's appearance or life choices, practice empathy. Recognize the diverse struggles women face daily, from financial worries to recovering from toxic relationships. Replace judgment with understanding and compassion.

5. Amplify Your Own Kind

Embrace the 'Shine Theory,' recognizing that elevating other women enhances the collective shine. Support your female counterparts actively, whether it's acknowledging their efforts in group projects, sharing commendations with colleagues, or celebrating their achievements.

6. Always Listen Attentively and Patiently

All women need a release during their tough times. Let her do some emotional venting if she really needs it. Sometimes we instantly start feeling better as soon as we talk about things that bother us. When a woman feels she's heard, her brain releases an important chemical that produces the feeling of relaxation. Make sure you don't interrupt her while she's venting about something; make eye contact if needed, or just nod your head to validate that you're interested in listening.

7. Say More than 'You're Pretty'

Go beyond surface compliments. While beauty is acknowledged, take responsibility as a woman to be a catalyst for other women's dreams. In business or personal spheres, recruit, train, and mentor. Remind fellow women that their worth transcends physical features, emphasizing their broader contributions to the world.

Author Bio

Julianne Williams is an author, a single mother, and a former healthcare executive who rises from depression and hopelessness to the President of a large privately owned company. Her bestselling books are about finding strength and inner light when life mistreats us. The chapters discuss her life struggle being a widow and a single mother but are also packed with inspirational statements and quotes to alter your perspective. She's on a mission to support young women who lost their husbands and trying to navigate the pressure of society. This ink-and-paper hug is a reminder for you to never lose hope, work hard, keep your chin up, and your chest out, and trust the timing.

CONNECT WITH JULIANNE WILLIAMS

www.juliannewilliams.com | www.facebook.com/BraveEnoughCommunity?mibextid=LQQJ4d | www.linkedin.com/in/julianne-williams-1aa76917 | Instagram: @Brave_Enough_Community

Francine Juhlin: Unleashing the Warrior Princess of Personal Change

In the heart of our December magazine, we bring you an inspiring tale of personal transformation and empowerment. Meet Francine Juhlin, the remarkable Warrior Princess of Personal Change, whose journey from self-doubt to unwavering determination is nothing short of extraordinary.

The Oy Syndrome to Warrior Princess

Francine Juhlin's story begins with what she affectionately calls the "Oy syndrome." "Oy, I'm so tired. Oy, I'm so broke. Oy, I hate my job." These were the refrains that echoed in her life, signaling the need for change. However, like many of us, Francine didn't have a clear starting point. She embarked on a winding path, gathering an eclectic array of knowledge along the way.

In 1983, she left her hometown of Chicago to join the Navy, where she honed her skills as an aircraft electrician. Her journey continued as she earned an electronics degree and worked as a Manufacturing Engineer. Yet, the military environment beckoned once more, leading Francine to join the Army National Guard and deploy to Iraq in 2004.

A Master of Transformation

After her deployment, Francine didn't rest on her laurels. She pursued her Master of Business Administration and worked as a civil servant for the Navy in Jacksonville, Florida. Her diverse experiences culminated in a unique approach to change management. Drawing inspiration from her Naval Aviation Enterprise Six Sigma Green Belt certification, she crafted the "6-Step Process of Personal Change," a transformative guide she now shares with the world.

Empowering the Next Generation

Francine's passion for change didn't stop at her own transformation. It evolved into a mission to empower the next generation of female leaders. She realized that leadership isn't confined to checklists or manuals; it's a journey of growth, resilience, and determination. Francine's commitment is to build strong leaders today, rather than fix broken women tomorrow. She aspires to lay a solid foundation for young leaders, nurturing their potential and instilling the mindset needed for success.

The Butterfly That Changed Everything

Central to Francine's mission is her book, "The Butterfly That Changed Everything." It's not your typical fairytale; it's a whimsical guide to self-discovery and personal growth. In a world often filled with uncertainty and self-doubt, this book serves as a beacon of hope. It's more than words on paper; it's a lifeline for those seeking transformation.

Within its pages, you'll find not only Francine's remarkable journey but also a roadmap—the 6-Step Process for Personal Change. This meticulously crafted guide empowers you to pave your path towards a brighter future, full of potential and promise.

Your Transformation Awaits

As you delve into "The Butterfly That Changed Everything," you'll uncover the keys to your personal empowerment and the path to designing your destiny. Francine invites you to embark on this extraordinary journey alongside her, unlocking the superhero within you.

Are you ready to embrace change, claim your transformation, and unleash your inner warrior? The time is now, and Francine Juhlin's book is your trusted guide to making it a reality. Join us on this thrilling adventure of self-discovery, growth, and empowerment.

In the warm embrace of Francine's story, we find inspiration, motivation, and the promise of a brighter future. This December, let the Warrior Princess of Personal Change guide you toward a life filled with warmth, love, and the joy of giving back.

FIND OUT MORE ABOUT FRANCINE'S MISSION

https://personalchangewarriors.com/

MENTAL

Health

8 WAYS ON HOW TO DISCUSS YOUR MENTAL HEALTH WITH OTHERS

Stan Popovich

Do you struggle with your mental health and have a difficult time getting the people you know to be more understanding? In some cases, your friends and family members could give you a hard time regarding your anxieties and fears.

As a result, here are eight suggestions on how to deal with the people you know regarding your mental health issues.

1. Listen to the professionals and not your friends: Your peers may mean well, but when it comes down to it, the professionals are aware of your circumstances more than anyone. A counselor knows what you are going through and can help you deal with your problems. When you have questions about your mental health, consult with a therapist.

2. Don't argue with others: It is important that you do not get into arguments with those who are giving you a rough time. Your number one priority is to get relief from your anxieties. It is not your job to worry about how others may view your circumstances. Your health is more important than what other people may think.

3. Your goal is to get better: Concentrate on how you can face your fears and anxieties. Don't waste your time arguing with your colleagues who are giving you a difficult time. This isn't a public relations event where you need to get approval from everyone. This is your life and you are the one suffering. Your main focus is to get better.

4. Ask your friends to learn about your situation: Explain to your peers that the best way for them to help you is to learn about your mental health issues. They could talk to a counselor, read some good books, or join a support group to better understand your situation.

5. Pick your friends wisely: Distance yourself from those who won't make an effort to help understand what you are going through. You need to surround yourself with positive and supportive people. If you have problems or issues with a particular person, you can always ask a counselor for advice.

6. You are not alone: It can be very frustrating to manage your fear-related issues when the people you know are on your case. Remember, you are not alone. There are millions of people around the world who struggle with their fears, anxieties, and depression.

7. Attend a mental health support group: There are many mental health awareness support groups in your area. Many hospitals, churches, and counselors in your area will be able to provide you with a list of these organizations. These groups will be aware of your situation and can give you additional advice regarding your problems.

8. You can't manage your anxieties all by yourself: Your fears, anxieties, and depression can be difficult to manage and more than likely you will need some direction. Many people think that they can overcome their mental health problems on their own. This is a mistake. A person should seek assistance to start the recovery process.

Biography

Stan is the author of "A Layman's Guide to Managing Fear" which will help you discover a variety of techniques that can drastically improve your mental health. For more information, please visit Stan's website at http://www.managingfear.com

GARDENING CAN HEAL YOUR SOUL

After 10 years I nearly gave up. I worked in a job that drained me, there was a toxic relationship, and I had to keep my family away due to my dad's mental disorder. I was all alone and extremely unhappy with myself. The funny thing was that I should have been happy because I had accomplished everything I had worked towards since school. I had finished university, went through teacher's training, was teaching university students myself, worked at a relatively small private school, and had my own apartment, car, and retirement fund. Still, I felt terrible. Stuck.

I certainly didn't like my work situation, being inside most of the day with often loud and squirmy kids was just not for me. I often caught myself gazing outside the window, longing to be outdoors alone in quietness. A lot of my former colleagues enjoyed their work, they found gratitude I could never find. The work drained me until I was almost gone. My private life was challenging too. There was no one to come home to and I had to stay away from my parents due to my dad's narcissistic personality disorder.

Nobody seemed to see my suffering and I needed something reliable, something I felt I had control over in my life. I controlled my food intake and worked out until I ended up with 43kg at a height of 1.68m. Obviously, I ran out of energy and my family doctor put a stop to it with the diagnosis of burnout. It was such a relief! Finally, somebody noticed and jumped in to help me.

I put myself into a mental hospital, but their way of treating my specific problems was not what I needed. After one month, I left and started searching. What do I want to do with my life? What is my passion? What do I need to be happy? Nature, gardening, farming, food, and healthy living have always been my fields of interest, so I became a WWOOFer. I started on a farm in Germany, where I quickly became the head gardener. Working outside all day, rain or shine, weeding, planting, harvesting, and cooking with the produce was the most impactful therapy no clinic had to offer. Becoming part of the farmer's family and living with other WWOOFers helped me to come out of my isolation. The walls started to come down and all the held-in emotions started to come out. I remember having so much rage, anger, and sadness inside of me, that all I could do not hurt anyone was to go digging, weeding, or walking. I was anything close to okay, but I was starting to heal. It's a very painful process that takes a lot of time. Over the years I have been in several therapies, but the one that brought me back to life was gardening. After a couple of months, I ventured onto a farm in Ireland where I was honored to take over and expand the kitchen garden, establish a food forest, and care for their various animals. Of course, it was a challenge and not always easy, but I started to find the real me. Planning the garden, planting seeds, starting seedlings, and seeing them grow was something almost sacred. Experiencing the time and effort it takes to grow food, make cheese from fresh milk, and bake bread, healed my issue with food. I became more aware of its value, and I didn't see food as the enemy anymore. Being active in the garden made me feel hungry and I just couldn't starve anymore. I knew that the food I had available around me was good food and that my body would be thankful for this good fuel I mostly grew or prepared myself. Of course, this process took over a year, but it has been a sustainable therapy. I learned real-life skills in real-life settings. Gardening didn't only become a hobby for me, it became a necessity. And then it became a business. Now I help women worldwide to grow their own kitchen garden to feed their family organic food and to pursue a healthy lifestyle. I am happy to pass on the gift of gardening.

INES BATTERTON

🌐 mynordicgarden.ca
in linkedin.com/in/ines-batterton-94214221a
f facebook.com/mynordicgarden/
📷 @my_nordic_garden

THE UNSPOKEN KEY TO LASTING RELATIONSHIPS: CULTIVATING A RELATIONSHIP WITH YOURSELF

Written by Marlène Gravenberch

As we navigate the labyrinth of relationships, one often-neglected truth emerges like a guiding star: the cornerstone of any relationship lies within our relationship with ourselves. It took me nearly six decades to decipher this simple yet profound reality: to foster healthy and meaningful connections, one must first cultivate a robust and intimate relationship with oneself, rooted in our deepest values.

Reflecting on my journey, I realize that had I grasped this wisdom earlier, it would have illuminated my path, offering clarity to set essential boundaries and nurture a foundation built on my values. Our values serve as the compass guiding our choices, actions, and aspirations, not merely in solitude but also in the vibrant tapestry of relationships we weave throughout our lives.

Understanding and embracing our values instills a profound sense of self-awareness. It's akin to laying the bedrock for the sanctuary of our being. When we are intimately acquainted with our values, we establish a solid framework upon which all our interactions and connections are built.

Articulating and demonstrating our values isn't merely an act of self-expression; it's a beacon that beckons like-minded souls. By authentically embodying our principles from the outset, we create a powerful filter. Those who resonate with our values are drawn closer, while those whose values misalign gradually fade into the periphery.

Imagine if, from a tender age, we instilled in our children the art of articulating their values—a language that transcends mere words. This foundation would be the cornerstone upon which they construct relationships—relationships not just with others but with themselves. By imparting this wisdom early on, we gift them the prowess to navigate the intricate maze of human connections based on shared values.

The significance of this insight reverberates across all facets of life, not just in personal but also in professional realms. In the workplace, aligning with a company whose values echo our own fosters a sense of belonging and purpose. It's within this harmony of values that our potential thrives, and the foundation for long-lasting professional relationships is laid.

While the societal narrative often emphasizes external connections, the intimate bond we forge with ourselves remains the bedrock of our existence. To know ourselves intimately is to wield the power of self-respect, self-love, and self-compassion—an arsenal that fortifies us against the storms of life.
As women, we've shouldered the weight of societal expectations, often relegating our own needs and values for the sake of conformity. Yet, the tides are shifting. We stand at the precipice of a new era, one where the anthem of self-discovery and empowerment resounds louder than ever.

Embracing our values, unabashedly and unapologetically, isn't just an act of self-care; it's an act of revolution—a revolution that ignites the flame of authenticity in our relationships, that reshapes the narrative of what it means to love and be loved.

So, to the women of tomorrow and the women of today who continue to script their narratives: let your values be the lighthouse guiding you through the labyrinth of relationships.

May you embark on the journey of self-discovery, for therein lies the key to forging relationships that resonate, endure, and flourish.
In the end, it's not just about finding the right relationship; it's about nurturing the most crucial one—the relationship with yourself. For therein lies the seed from which every other connection blooms.

leadership-refocused.com
linkedin.com/in/marl%C3%A8ne-gravenberch-5655a61a/
/MMIGraRog
@marlenegravenberch

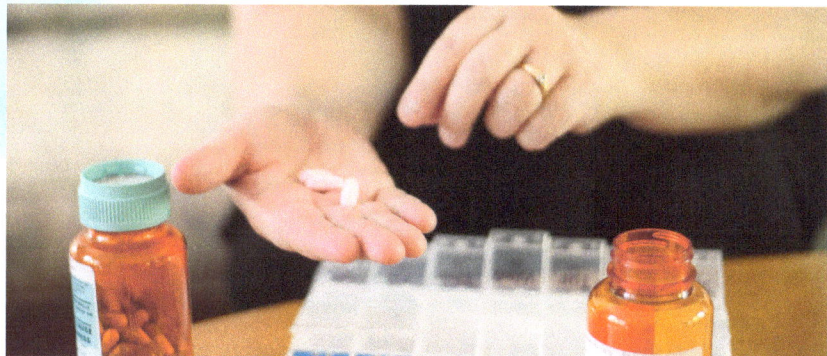

When Personal and Professional Worlds Collide: My Journey from Dementia Specialist to Family Caregiver

By Lizette Cloete

Have you ever experienced profound anger and frustration in your life? Whether it be at work, at home, or when cornered like an animal and wanting to lash out in anger, just to escape?

I have. As an occupational therapist and a dementia specialist, navigating the healthcare system as a daughter of dementia makes me angry.

Why does it make me angry, you might wonder?

Because it is failing both the patient and the family caregiver, putting up unnecessary barriers to care, frustrating the people who are navigating more than 17 different systems just to be told they need to go back to where they started.

And I have 30 years of experience in healthcare. I know the system. I know the "tips and tricks" and should have been able to negotiate this easily.

And I didn't.

Three years ago, when I noticed my father experiencing changes, I said something to the healthcare providers.

But it took me an additional year to convince his primary care that something was wrong. This was eye-opening for me.

And then it took another year to even get an appointment with the specialist.

I had high hopes for this specialty appointment since this is the only cognitive/memory health center in my State.

But I left there disappointed. We had a diagnosis. But, other than that, crickets.

A follow-up appointment, sure. One year later.

No community resources were provided for cognitive loss. No online resources were provided for cognitive loss. No brochure or handout was provided for cognitive loss.

I am trying to be gracious. I am a healthcare professional. And I was open and forthright about that.

But my dad, who received a life-changing diagnosis, was provided absolutely no support. No resources, no information. Nothing. Crickets.

Why is this important? Because ⅓ adults over 65 have some form of dementia. And the older you are, the more likely you will develop it.

Roslyn Carter was quoted to have said: "There are only four kinds of people in the world. Those who have been caregivers. Those who are currently caregivers. Those who will be caregivers, and those who will need a caregiver."

And if you are a woman between the ages of 40-65 years old, you are likely one of these 4 kinds of people.

Because 66% of caregivers are female. And of those, 1/3 are daughters. And of female caregivers, about 60% are still working 30+ hours per week.

This prompted me to change the focus of the fledgling business I had started in 2020 called "Think Different Dementia" from focusing on professional caregivers to family caregivers.

What am I creating? I am creating an uplifting community for dementia caregivers. A safe, and positive space for family caregivers to find reliable education, community, and coaching, so that you can navigate a caregiving journey without stress, burnout and redeem your time, creating moments of joy.

If your loved one has been diagnosed with dementia, you are a family caregiver if you answer yes to any of these: you take someone to appointments; you help with grocery shopping, household chores, or maintenance; you provide personal care; you set up medications or administer medications: you help navigate the healthcare system; you provide emotional or social connection; you help pay the bills or feed a pet.

Many people do not even recognize that they are a family caregiver, and when that occurs, it makes a difficult journey even more overwhelming. My purpose and passion are to help families recognize their power in caregiving, to change the narrative related to dementia caregiving, and to forge an easier way for people to live, laugh, and love through this special time in their lives, redeeming their time.

To connect with Lizette, contact her at www.thinkdifferentdementia.com/contact or listen to the podcast Dementia Caregiving for Families on all the normal channels.

www.dementiacaregivingmadeeasy.com | www.thinkdifferentdementia.com | www.facebook.com/lcloete2/ |
podcasts.apple.com/us/podcast/dementia-caregiving-for-families/id1716187550 | www.linkedin.com/in/lizette-cloete-8a39821aa/

Cynthia Concordia: Inspiring Transformation and Fulfillment

In a world teeming with life's complexities, Cynthia Encinas-Concordia shines as a guiding light of transformation, empowerment, and the pursuit of dreams. A transformational life coach, published author, podcast host, mother, and grandmother, Cynthia's journey has been marked by a relentless commitment to inspire others to create the lives they love.

A Career of Diversity and Human Connection

Cynthia's professional path led her to the hallowed halls of the World Bank as a Human Resource practitioner. Her role brought her face-to-face with diverse groups of people, allowing her to develop a profound understanding of human dynamics. Her career at the World Bank was a fusion of knowledge, experience, and skills that would later become the cornerstone of her life's work.

A Calling to Make a Difference

Cynthia's professional journey intersected with her personal life, revealing a profound calling. Through her own life's twists and turns, she recognized the power of making a positive impact on others. This realization became the catalyst for her mission: to inspire and empower individuals to unlock their full potential and craft lives they truly love.

"I had the best opportunity—through my life journey, to see the value of making a positive impact on others' lives. I felt a calling to make a difference by inspiring others and creating awareness to empower people to unlock their full potential and create a life they love. I am results-oriented and passionate about personal growth and mindset mastery."

Leaving Footprints for the Future

For Cynthia, this mission is not just about the present; it's about the legacy she leaves for future generations. She seeks to inspire and empower the young generation to carry the torch, to continue making a profound impact on the world.

"With me fulfilling my purpose, I am now leaving my footprints so the young generation may be inspired and continue what we are doing – making an impact in this world."

CYNTHIA CONCORDIA

🌐 www.dreamtorise.info

Dream to Rise: Illuminating Lives

Cynthia's vision culminated in the founding of Dream to Rise, LLC, a platform that encapsulates her unwavering commitment to transformation and personal growth. Through Dream to Rise, she offers coaching, guidance, and inspiration to those yearning for change and fulfillment.

A Published Legacy

Cynthia's journey as an author is equally impressive. Her books, including "My Journey Into Becoming," "Overcoming Self-Sabotage," and the eagerly awaited "Dream to Rise Anthology" (scheduled for release in December 2023), reflect her dedication to sharing her wisdom and experiences with the world.

Creating a Life You Love

In Cynthia's own words, "Join me on this incredible journey of self-discovery, and let's create the life you've always dreamed of. I want you to live your dreams and welcome each day full of gratitude, saying, 'Life is great!'"

As we eagerly await the release of the "Dream to Rise Anthology," Cynthia Concordia's life story, and her unwavering dedication to empowering others, serve as a reminder that transformation and fulfillment are within reach for us all. Her footprints pave the way for a brighter future, where individuals from all walks of life can embrace their potential and live a life they truly love.

Grace Clarke: Illuminating Inner Light Through Art and Storytelling

In the world of creativity and self-discovery, Grace Clarke stands as a shining example of an artist, author, and mother who channels her inner light into her work. Born in the suburbs of Philadelphia, PA, Grace's life journey has taken her to various places, but she now calls Tampa, FL, her home. Here, amidst the tranquility of her surroundings, she finds inspiration to create art and tell stories that touch the soul.

A Mission to Shine Authentically

Grace Clarke's mission is beautifully simple yet profound: "I simply wish to shine brightly and authentically as myself so that others may do the same." This heartfelt purpose infuses her art, her writing, and her daily life, resonating with those who encounter her work.

"From the Stars Above": A Labor of Love

Grace's book, "From the Stars Above," is a testament to her inner exploration and creative spirit. It emerged from a period of isolation, during which she delved deep into the recesses of her soul. The story, which appeared in her mind with unwavering clarity, was transcribed with unmatched ferocity.

The journey of creation was a unique one. Grace swiftly translated her thoughts onto paper, crafting the initial draft of the book. However, the process then evolved, as she channeled her artistic talents into hand-painting the illustrations that grace its pages. Over a year's time, these paintings came to life, each stroke of the brush a reflection of her inner world.

A Precious Journey to Share

The book's first mock-up, created during this intimate and labor-intensive process, holds a special place in Grace's heart. Now, the world holds in its hands the very first version released into the wild of published works. It's a labor of love, a testament to her journey of self-discovery, and a gift to those who encounter it.

"From the Stars Above": A Tale of Inner Light

"From the Stars Above" is a short story suitable for all ages. Grace Clarke's intuitive art adorns its pages, giving life to a tale of a princess from the stars. This princess embarks on a quest to rediscover her inner light, a journey that ultimately reminds us all of the brilliance within ourselves.

In the vibrant, hand-painted imagery and the soulful storytelling, Grace invites readers to reconnect with their inner spark, to embark on their own pathways of self-discovery. Her work is not just a book; it's an invitation to explore the depths of one's soul, embrace authenticity, and shine brightly in a world that often seeks to dim our inner light.

As we immerse ourselves in the world of "From the Stars Above" and Grace Clarke's creations, we find a guiding light—an artist, author, and mother whose mission is to inspire us all to illuminate our inner selves and live authentically. Grace's work is a reminder that, like the princess from the stars, we too can rediscover our inner light and radiate it for the world to see.

Leigh Lincoln: Crafting Stories of Redemption and Discovery

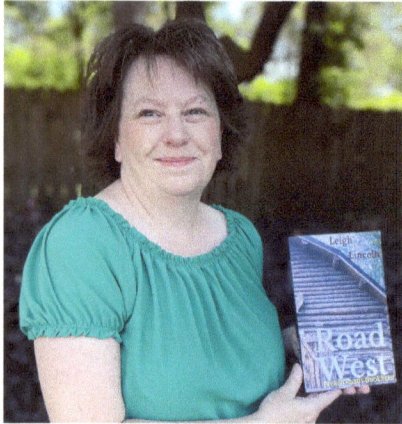

In the realm of literature, Leigh Lincoln is an author whose narratives resonate deeply with the human experience. With a passion for storytelling that touches hearts and provokes thoughtful reflection, she has carved a path that intertwines her love for writing with her dedication to advocating for the homeless and those living in poverty. Her journey as an author is a testament to her commitment to making people ponder the choices they make, how they treat others, and the importance of empathy.

A Life Devoted to Advocacy

Leigh Lincoln's journey has led her down a remarkable path of advocacy for the homeless and impoverished communities. For over three decades, she has dedicated herself to making a difference in the lives of those in need. Her first novel, "Road Home," was born from this tireless work. It serves as a thought-provoking mirror to society, challenging readers to consider how they live, treat others, and desire to be treated.

The Broken Roads Series: Picking up the Pieces

Leigh's literary exploration continues with the "Broken Roads Series." Comprising novels like "Road to Freedom," "Finding the Real Road," and "The Road West," these stories delve into the idea that life doesn't always follow the path we envision. Instead, we encounter unexpected twists and turns, forcing us to gather the fragments of our existence and move forward.

A Personal Glimpse: "Lost Father"

Leigh's most recent novel, "Lost Father," stands as her most personal work to date. It delves into the profound journey of a man grappling with the aftermath of an unexpected pregnancy. "The Path to Family Series" will shine a light on the emotional and hopeful tale of adoption from the perspectives of those involved. Through this series, Leigh shares her own deeply personal adoption experience with her readers, inviting them to connect with the emotional depths of the narrative.

Inspiration Through Conversation

Leigh is not just an author; she's a voice that encourages others to find their own. Through her interviews on various podcasts and radio shows, she strives to inspire individuals to discover their unique voices, explore the world, and never shy away from meaningful conversations. Her passion lies in crafting novels that resonate with readers on a profound emotional level, aiming to uplift, inspire, and provoke introspection.

A Compassionate Mission

What sets Leigh Lincoln apart is her commitment to giving back. A portion of the proceeds from her novels directly supports charities that serve the homeless and impoverished communities. Her writing is a reflection of her compassionate spirit, a means to make a positive impact on those in need.

A Journey of Discovery

While Leigh may be a relatively new presence in the world of writing, her journey is far from complete. Her love for travel, painting, and hiking fuels her continuous exploration of life's wonders. As she embarks on her own journey of discovery, she continues to craft stories that touch the soul and inspire others to embark on their paths of self-discovery and redemption.

Leigh Lincoln's work is a testament to the power of literature to provoke thought, inspire change, and make a lasting impact on the lives of those who read her words. Through her storytelling, she invites us all to reflect on our own journeys, the choices we make, and the profound impact of empathy and compassion in our world.

HER
AND NOW

High-Performance Habits for Mompreneurs: Balancing Motherhood and Entrepreneurship

Angela Bell

Mompreneurs are those amazing women who have successfully embraced both motherhood and entrepreneurship. Juggling the demands of raising a family while running a business can be challenging, but there are specific high-performance habits that can help mompreneurs not only survive but thrive in their dual roles. In this article, we will explore seven key habits that can empower mompreneurs to achieve success and fulfillment.

Time Blocking:
One of the most crucial habits for mompreneurs is effective time management. Time blocking involves dividing the day into specific blocks of time dedicated to different tasks. By creating a structured schedule, mompreneurs can ensure that they allocate sufficient time to both their business and family responsibilities. This helps in maintaining a sense of order and preventing overwhelm.

Prioritization and Delegation:
Understanding the difference between urgent and important tasks is essential for mompreneurs. Prioritizing tasks allows them to focus on what truly matters, both in their business and family life. Additionally, successful mompreneurs master the art of delegation. Delegating tasks to reliable team members or seeking support from family and friends can lighten the workload, providing more time and energy for strategic business decisions and quality family time.

Self-Care:
Taking care of oneself is often overlooked in the busy lives of mompreneurs. However, maintaining physical and mental well-being is crucial for sustained high performance. Regular exercise, sufficient sleep, and moments of relaxation are all vital components of self-care. When mompreneurs prioritize their health, they are better equipped to handle the challenges of entrepreneurship and parenting.

Goal Setting and Planning:
Mompreneurs thrive on setting clear, achievable goals for both their personal and professional lives. By establishing short-term and long-term objectives, they can stay focused and motivated. Breaking down larger goals into smaller, manageable tasks makes the journey more attainable. Creating a comprehensive business plan and setting realistic milestones help mompreneurs track their progress and make informed decisions.

Flexibility and Adaptability:
Entrepreneurship is inherently unpredictable, and motherhood brings its own set of uncertainties. Successful mompreneurs cultivate a mindset of flexibility and adaptability to navigate the ever-changing landscape of business and family life. Being open to adjusting plans, learning from setbacks, and embracing change enables them to stay resilient and maintain a positive outlook.

Effective Communication:
Clear and effective communication is a cornerstone of success for mompreneurs. Whether it's discussing expectations with family members or conveying ideas to business partners, strong communication skills are vital. Mompreneurs must be able to express their needs, set boundaries, and articulate their vision for both their business and family. This fosters a supportive environment and ensures that everyone is on the same page.

Continuous Learning:
The world of entrepreneurship is dynamic and ever-evolving. Mompreneurs who commit to continuous learning stay ahead of industry trends and acquire new skills. Whether it's attending workshops, reading books, or seeking mentorship, the pursuit of knowledge is a powerful habit that propels mompreneurs toward success. By staying curious and adaptable, they position themselves as leaders in their field.

Being a mompreneur is a unique and rewarding journey that requires a combination of strategic planning, adaptability, and self-care. By cultivating high-performance habits such as time blocking, prioritization, self-care, goal setting, flexibility, effective communication, and continuous learning, mompreneurs can strike a harmonious balance between their roles as mothers and entrepreneurs. These habits not only contribute to personal fulfillment but also empower mompreneurs to build successful businesses while nurturing their families.

www.inspirednprofitablemompreneur.com | www.instagram.com/i.am.angelabell | www.facebook.com/angela.bell.3597 | www.facebook.com/groups/inspiredandprofitablemompreneurs

Your Journey: Navigating Life and Business

By Ashley Pakulski

Alright, let's dive into your journey – not just in life but also in business. Life's a bit like a rollercoaster, and business adds its own twists, right? For many of us, mental health, addiction, and the hustle of business are all part of the ride. But here's the deal – your journey, with its mix of challenges and victories, is what makes it uniquely yours.

Embracing Life's Mix: Handling Challenges in Business and Beyond

Life can throw curveballs, and business has its ups and downs. Mental health and addiction might be part of that journey, and that's perfectly okay. The unexpected turns? They are what makes your story yours! Running a business isn't just about that. It's about rebuilding your identity and stepping into your higher version of self.

In those uncertain moments, remember you're not alone. Many have walked similar paths, facing struggles that aren't signs of weakness but rather moments of strength. Your journey is waiting for you to paint it with courage, hope, and a vision for a brighter future for both you and your business.

Finding Strength Inside: A Shared Struggle We All Know

In those quiet moments where doubts creep in – in life and business – know that there's a whole bunch of us grappling with the same stuff. We're all works in progress, learning and growing together. Embrace the idea that becoming who you are is just as important as where you're taking your business.

Morning Routines: Simple Steps for a Productive Day in Business and Life

Now, let's talk about morning routines – your secret weapon for a better day, both personally and in business. It's not just about going through the motions; it's like creating a little morning routine for yourself and your business. Doing some breathwork and meditation, taking a moment to reflect, or just enjoying some peace – these small acts are like planting seeds of positivity for your day.

Taking Care of You and Your Business: Simple Self-Care for the Win

Imagine this – your morning routine is like a tiny act of self-care, setting the tone for both your personal life and your business endeavors. It's choosing to start your day on a positive note, reminding yourself that you matter and today is going to be okay – for you and your business.

Your Inner Journey: More Than Just a Destination for Personal and Business Growth

Let's talk about your inner world – the thoughts, feelings, and hopes inside you, and how they connect with your business. This journey is shared by all of us who are entrepreneurs. We're figuring things out, dealing with our struggles, and celebrating victories – both personal and professional. Remember, it's okay not to have everything figured out; we're all learning as we go.

Wishing You Brighter Mornings, Stronger Businesses, and Balanced Days Ahead

So, here's to you – embracing your journey, finding hope in the whispers of each new day, and managing the hustle of your business with grace. Your story is yours to tell, and even in the simple things, you're making strides towards a brighter, happier you – both personally and in your business. Wishing you mornings filled with positivity, businesses filled with growth, and days filled with strength.

facebook.com/groups/mompreneurssuccesscircle/   @theashleypakulski

REVOLUTIONIZING HEALTHCARE:
BLOCKCHAIN AND NFTS AT THE FOREFRONT

With the year coming to a close and a new one on the horizon, we can think of our health. How can technology help us continue to thrive for many years to come? I'll be breaking down such possibilities in this article.

Blockchain and Non-Fungible Tokens (NFTs) are two big new technologies that have come out in a world where technology changes quickly. Even though many believe this technology is tied only to cryptocurrencies and digital art, its possible use in the medical field is getting more and more attention. When you combine blockchain's decentralized, secure, and open nature with the unique identification features of NFTs, you get a game-changing way to manage medical records and patient data, especially in global healthcare.

Blockchain in Healthcare: A New Era for Managing Data

Blockchain technology gives data management security and openness that have yet to be seen in this field. With the blockchain, this means keeping patient records safe and consistent across all practices within the medical field. Because blockchain is decentralized, medical records will not isolated in one place. Because of this decentralization, it makes it less likely that data will be lost, stolen, or changed.

Also, blockchain's built-in audit trail feature makes it possible to see who accessed and changed the medical records. This transparency allows people to trust the system more, ensuring patient data is handled honestly and responsibly.

NFTs and Medical Records for Individuals

The idea of NFTs, which are digital tokens that show ownership of a unique item or asset, can be used in medical records in a new way. Each patient's medical history can be "tokenized" into an NFT. NFTs ensure that each patient's medical data is unique, can be identified, and is securely linked to that patient only. This NFT would be like a digital key that lets you access the patient's medical history.

This method ensures that medical records are portable and easily accessible, which is very important for patients who travel abroad. In a medical emergency abroad, healthcare providers can access the patient's medical history through the blockchain if the patient gives permission, allowing for timely and accurate medical care.

Universal Medical Records: A Framework for Thought

Imagine a system for all medical records based on blockchain and NFT technology. Every person has a personal NFT-linked medical record that can be accessed from anywhere in the world. This record has their medical history, including allergies, surgeries, current treatments, and medicines they are taking.

If a patient gives permission, their healthcare provider can look at this universal record when they go to the doctor or the hospital. Any new medical information created, like a prescription, a diagnostic test result, or notes from a visit to the doctor, is added to the blockchain immediately and safely.

Potential to Save Lives in Medical Emergencies Abroad

This system has enormous effects on the real world, especially for travelers. Think about a tourist who has a medical emergency while they are traveling. Language barriers, not knowing enough about local medicine, and not having access to a patient's medical history can complicate things, leading to a wrong diagnosis or treatment.

With permission from the patient or their emergency contact, a blockchain-based universal medical record lets doctors and nurses in any country see the patient's medical history immediately. Quick access to accurate medical data can save lives by allowing doctors to decide what treatments to use in an emergency.

Challenges and Things to Think About

There are problems with such a system, even though the benefits could be huge. These include protecting patients' privacy, keeping track of their permissions to access their data, and connecting various healthcare systems worldwide to a single blockchain network. Global regulatory frameworks and standards must also exist for this kind of system to work.

Final Thoughts

Using blockchain technology and NFTs in the medical field, mainly to keep track of medical records, could completely change how healthcare is provided worldwide. It can make medical care safer and more effective, especially for people in foreign places. As technology improves, policymakers, tech developers, and people in the healthcare industry need to work together to solve problems and make the global healthcare system safer and more connected.

Written By:
Lauren Weiss

+1(316)530-1142
www.cyclealign.com
hello@cyclealign.com

ARE YOU READY FOR CONTENT DAY?

EmpowerHer Content Day!

February, 22, 2024
Tivoli Village
At the El Dorado Cantina
Restaurant & Bar

430

EL DORADO CANTINA
RESTAURANT & BAR

For more details and to get your TICKET, go to SheRisesStudios.com

HOLIDAY
Features

What Christmas Means To Me

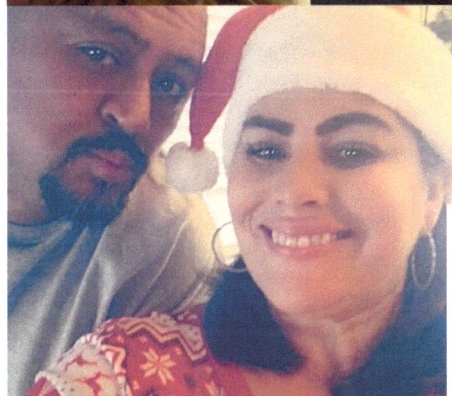

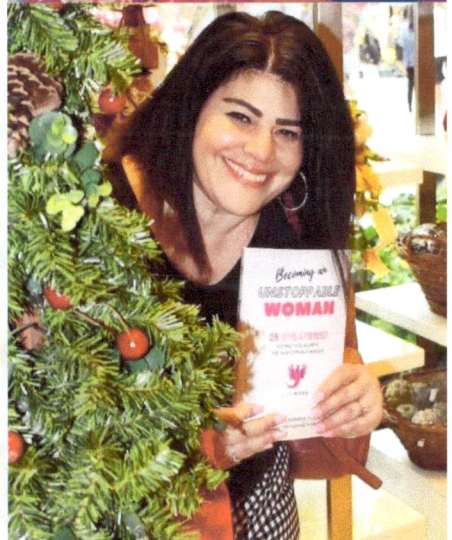

Christmas time, also known as the holiday season, is such an incredible way to end a year and begin a new one. Throughout the year we get caught up in the daily grind. Sometimes we're overwhelmed and stressed and we forget to focus on what matters most. When I think of Christmas time it reminds me of magic, hope, faith, love, generosity, traditions, family, connections and so much more. I love spending time with all my family, embracing them all, and celebrating each and every moment together. Life is the biggest gift of all! So let's not take it for granted, not even for a split second. The holiday season is just more of a reason to be reminded daily how important our health, wealth, well-being, family, faith, and friends are. Hold on to it tight and don't let it go. It is a wonderful life if you allow it to be and the good news is Christmas time is when you get to appreciate and experience even more and with the whole world. How cool is that? Most of the world celebrates this one holiday in love and peace and that is a big Christmas gift too! So make this holiday season your best one yet, not with materialistic items but with love and traditions, and make the magic happen in your own homes, spread the holiday cheer wherever you go!

XOXO,
Hanna Olivas

www.sherisesstudios.com
www.facebook.com/sherisesstudios
@hannaolivasofficial

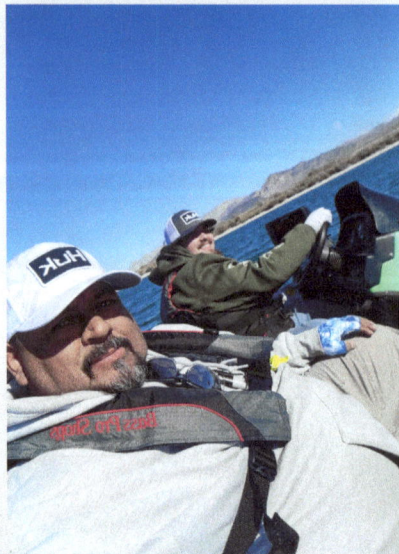

Written by Ron Billings

Dear Mom and Dad,

As I sit down to write this, I am overwhelmed with gratitude and a profound sense of love. There are moments in life when we need to pause and express the depth of our feelings, and today is one of those days. So, here's a heartfelt note to both of you, my pillars of strength and the architects of my life.

I find it difficult to put into words the impact you have had on my life. From the earliest memories of childhood to the challenges of adulthood, your unwavering support has been my constant. Mom, your warm hugs, and Dad, your reassuring words – these have been the anchors that have kept me grounded in the stormy seas of life.

Reflecting on the journey we've shared brings tears to my eyes – tears of joy, gratitude, and an overwhelming sense of love. You've been more than just parents; you've been my mentors, my confidants, and my friends. In every trial and triumph, you stood by me, offering guidance without judgment and love without conditions.

Mom, your nurturing spirit has been a source of comfort in times of distress. Your ability to turn an ordinary day into something special with a simple smile or a homemade meal is a testament to your incredible strength. You've taught me the importance of kindness, resilience, and the power of a mother's love.

Dad, your wisdom has been my guiding light. Your quiet strength and unwavering belief in me have fueled my confidence to face the world. The lessons you've imparted, both through words and actions, have shaped my character and instilled in me the values of hard work, integrity, and perseverance.

Together, you've created a home that is more than just walls and a roof; it's a sanctuary of love, laughter, and acceptance. The memories we've built – from family dinners to heartfelt conversations on the porch – are the threads that weave the fabric of my identity.

As I navigate the complexities of life, I realize that your influence is imprinted on every decision, every success, and every failure. You've given me the wings to fly and the roots to stay connected to my essence. The challenges I've faced were less daunting because I knew you were there, cheering me on from the sidelines.

Today, I want to express my deepest gratitude for the sacrifices you've made, the lessons you've taught, and the love you've showered upon me. It's not just about the big moments but the countless little ones – the bedtime stories, the scraped knees you bandaged, and the quiet moments of understanding.

I am who I am because of you. Your love has been a beacon, illuminating the path of my life. I may not have always said it, but every achievement, every smile, and every step forward has been a silent acknowledgment of the love and support you've given me.

So, dear Mom and Dad, this is not just a letter; it's a monument of gratitude, a testament to the profound impact you've had on my life. Thank you for being my guiding stars, my greatest allies, and my eternal source of love.

With all my love,

Your Son.

sherisesstudios.com

THIS SEASON IS FOR BELIEVING

By Prudence Hatchett

We are currently living in the most magical time of the year. The time when cheer and glee are all around, including endless sweets and a lot of ho-ho-ho's. Joy and happiness are graciously spreading in the air. To be honest, December is my favorite time of the year because it contains my birthday, Christmas, and New Year's Eve. So I get pretty amped up during this time of year and I love every minute of it. But I have a secret. December is the time that I get to relax, reminisce, and rejuvenate from the previous months. Don't get me wrong, this does not mean that I work myself to the bone during these previous months because I believe in rest and recharging. This is how I keep my emotions balanced, along with other coping skills. But for me, it does mean that December is for believing in the most enchanted possibilities. You see, I never wait until January to make meaningful plans. Oh, I enjoy making New Year's resolutions like the next person but mainly in theory and tradition. Setting myself up for success in the new year takes preparation, planning, and guts! I prepare and plan for what I know to do with the resources that I can access on my own. But there is a secret ingredient that can't be seen, smelled, or touched and it is called believing. Believing in myself, believing in my skills, and believing that I have something valuable to give to the world. Sometimes on the preparation and planning journey, we may get hit with some unexpected twists and turns. This may lead to discouragement and disappointment and you will need something to help you get past this hump. This "something" is you. If you do not believe in yourself, your product, or your team no one else will. Now, I don't believe in having your head in the clouds. Meaning, it's ok to acknowledge the setbacks and disappointments. In fact, I recommend it. But I also recommend finding that reset button and not sinking deeper and deeper into the abyss. Believing can be the secret ingredient to what aids you in the problem-solving process, increases creativity and imagination, or promotes out-of-the-box thinking. Sometimes believing can be hard at first because you can't see it, and neither can other people. Not seeing tangible objects or quick results can lead to fear and self-criticism if you are not carefully paying attention to your thoughts. Or even worse, other people will start to criticize and that can feel heavy. So what is believing? In essence, believing is something you can feel, something you can think, and something that is in your heart that will motivate you to keep going. And I want to motivate you to keep going! Keep working on your goals and keep believing in yourself. So this season, hit that reset button, take time to rest, and enjoy the holidays. Allow this time of year to stimulate your hope, inspiration, and determination. It all starts with believing in yourself. Be open to change and learning new things. Get ready to step out of your comfort zone, take action, and believe in the enchanted. After all, this is the most magical time of the year.

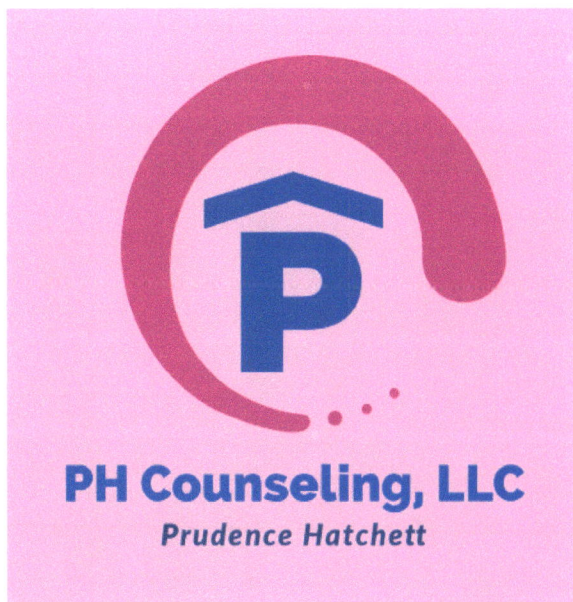

PH Counseling, LLC
Prudence Hatchett

LET'S
CELEBRATE

INAUGURAL BOOK SIGNING SUCCESS —— Cheryl Field

The Barnes & Noble bookstore in Newington, New Hampshire, became a hub of local excitement and appreciation during a recent book signing event featuring Cheryl Field, MSN, RN, CRRN. Cheryl, a cherished native of New Hampshire, brought her wealth of experience in senior care spanning an impressive 35 years to the forefront with her book, "Prepared! A Healthcare Guide for Aging Adults."

The anticipation surrounding this event was palpable, drawing in a robust crowd eager to glean insights from Cheryl's extensive expertise in senior care. As a revered figure in the local community, Cheryl's commitment to the welfare of aging adults resonated deeply with attendees, and the bookstore buzzed with enthusiastic conversation and anticipation.

The event saw an impressive turnout, with an engaged audience eager to connect with Cheryl and gain valuable insights from her book. The ambiance was one of warmth and camaraderie, as Cheryl welcomed each guest with a genuine appreciation for their presence.

"Prepared! A Healthcare Guide for Aging Adults" struck a chord with attendees, as it speaks directly to the challenges and concerns faced by those navigating the complexities of senior care. Cheryl's compassionate and knowledgeable approach shone through as she personalized each of the 16 copies sold during the event. Her dedication to ensuring that every reader felt a personal connection to the book was evident in the heartfelt messages she inscribed within the covers.

Attendees were not merely purchasing a book; they were engaging with a resource crafted with care and expertise, tailored to address the nuanced needs of aging adults and their caregivers. Cheryl's guidance and insights resonated deeply with those present, fostering a sense of empowerment and preparedness amidst the challenges of healthcare for seniors.

The atmosphere at Barnes & Noble echoed conversations about the significance of proactive healthcare planning and the invaluable wisdom imparted by Cheryl's book. Guests eagerly discussed and exchanged thoughts on topics ranging from caregiving techniques to navigating the healthcare system, enriched by Cheryl's guidance and personal anecdotes shared during the event.

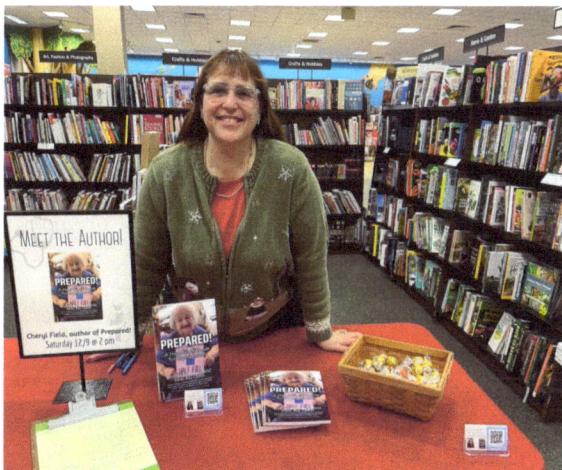

🌐 www.cheryl.field.com
📘 www.facebook.com/cheryl.field.18
in www.linkedin.com/in/cherylfield1621

The success of the book signing event was a testament not only to Cheryl's profound knowledge and dedication but also to the pressing need for accessible, comprehensive resources in the realm of senior care. Her genuine passion for improving the lives of aging adults and their caregivers resonated profoundly with the community, leaving a lasting impact on all who attended.

As the event drew to a close, attendees departed with more than just a signed copy of "Prepared! A Healthcare Guide for Aging Adults." They left with a newfound sense of empowerment, armed with practical knowledge and heartfelt advice from a local luminary whose impact on senior care extends far beyond the pages of her book.

Cheryl Field's book signing event at Barnes & Noble in Newington, NH, was not only a celebration of her accomplishments but also a reminder of the invaluable role that compassionate expertise plays in navigating the intricate landscape of senior healthcare. Her dedication to serving the community and empowering individuals in their healthcare journeys reverberated throughout the event, leaving attendees inspired and enriched with newfound insights

Beyond the Smile: Cindy Witteman's Unveiling of Life's Imperfections

Featuring Cindy Witteman

In the vibrant city of San Antonio, Texas, resides a remarkable woman, Cindy Witteman, whose multifaceted identity encompasses entrepreneurship, literature, media, philanthropy, and a commitment to uplifting single parents. A proud business owner, 3x Best Selling Author, TV Show host, and founder of Driving Single Parents Inc., Cindy is a force of positivity, but her forthcoming book, "Beyond the Smile," reveals a deeper, more authentic narrative.

Despite the polished exterior showcased on her TV Show, "Little Give," or the poised demeanor during public speeches, Cindy opens up about the imperfections that persist in her life. "Beyond the Smile" serves as a mirror, reflecting the moments of self-doubt and the challenges that often accompany success. It's a testament to resilience and the transformative power of hard work and dedication.

Cindy, the CEO of Driving Single Parents Inc., embodies a dedication to giving back that goes beyond providing reliable vehicles. Celebrating its 6th year, the non-profit has been a beacon of hope for single-parent families. By offering vehicles at no cost, the organization empowers parents to overcome obstacles and turn their struggles into success stories.

Cindy Witteman's journey is deeply rooted in her experience as a former single parent and proud stepmother of a blended family consisting of six kids, one grandson, and two granddaughters. Her genuine passion for helping others is evident in the impact Driving Single Parents Inc. has had on countless lives.

Beyond her charitable endeavors, Cindy wears the hat of an avid beekeeper, a testament to her diverse interests. Her ability to balance the roles of entrepreneur, author, speaker, and TV show host showcases the dynamism of a woman dedicated to making a positive impact.

Adding another layer to her already impressive repertoire, Cindy is the host of the "Is Manifesting Bullshit?" Podcast. This show is dedicated to sifting fact from fiction, helping listeners uncover the secrets of effective manifestation. In her unique style, Cindy explores the realities of manifesting and provides insights that separate hype from genuine practices.

In "Beyond the Smile," Cindy promises readers an intimate look into her life, dispelling the myth of perfection and offering inspiration to those navigating their own journeys. The book is set to release in early 2024, poised to become a source of motivation for anyone striving to overcome challenges and embrace personal growth.

To catch glimpses of Cindy's uplifting work and witness ordinary people doing extraordinary things on her TV Show, "Little Give," visit LittleGive.com. The platform serves as a testament to the transformative power of small acts of kindness and the impact they can have on individuals and communities.

As Cindy Witteman continues to shape the narrative of success, "Beyond the Smile" stands as a beacon of authenticity, reminding us that even those who seemingly have it all face their own battles. Cindy's story is not just a celebration of achievements but a testament to the strength found in vulnerability and the unwavering spirit of giving back to the community she cherishes.

Find out more by visiting her website:
CFViews.com

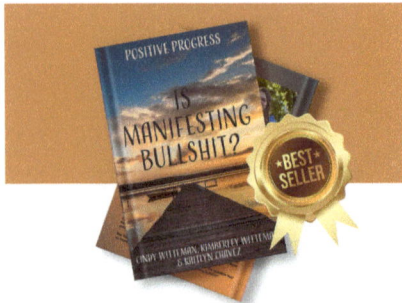

Best Seller in
WOMEN & BUSINESS
AVAILABLE ON amazon.com

CFViews.com
DrivingSingleParents.org

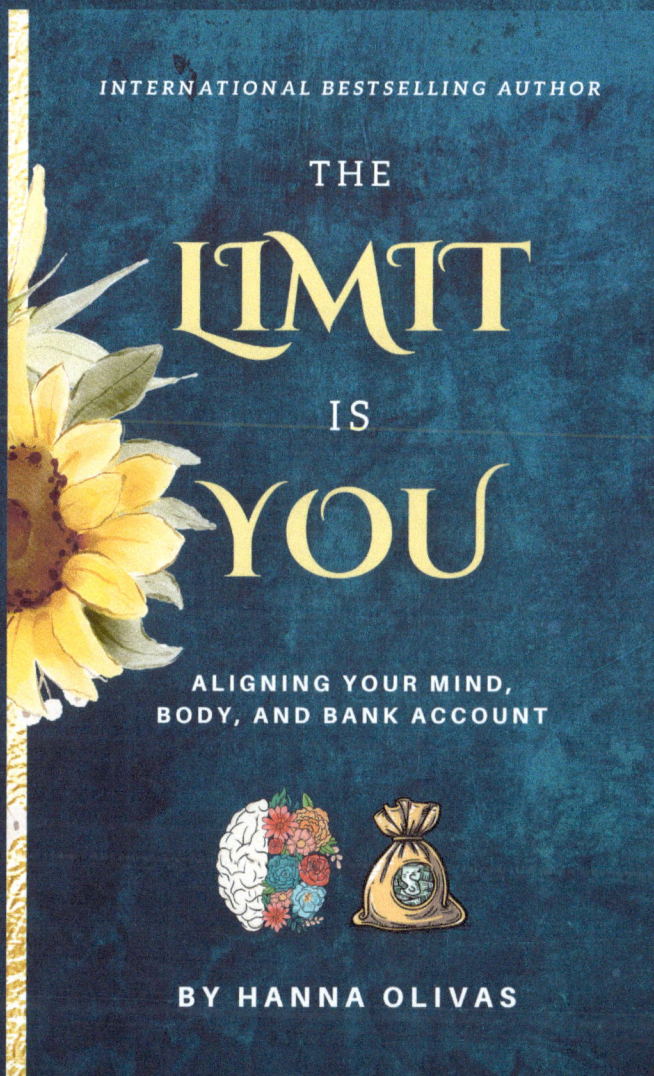

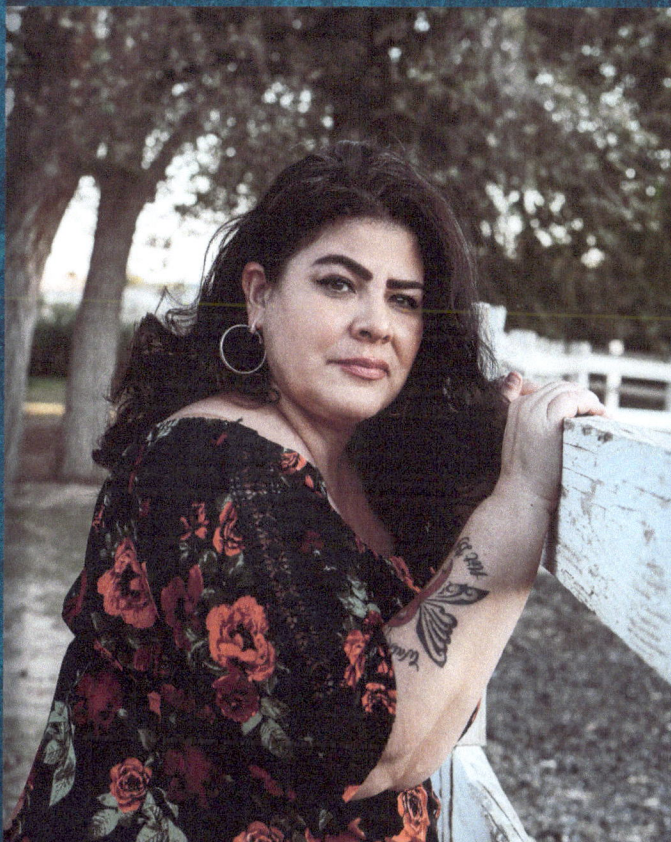

www.ingramcontent.com/pod-product-compliance
Lightning Source LLC
Chambersburg PA
CBHW050913210326
41597CB00002B/102